# GRADUS

## MUSIC ANTHOLOGY

## BOOK I

# GRADUS

## MUSIC ANTHOLOGY

---

## BOOK I

---

## by Leo Kraft

PROFESSOR OF MUSIC, QUEENS COLLEGE OF THE CITY UNIVERSITY OF NEW YORK

W·W·Norton & Company·Inc·New York

to the memory of Paul Klapper

Library of Congress Cataloging in Publication Data

Kraft, Leo.
  Gradus.

  Includes bibliographies.
  — —Music anthology.
  1. Music—Theory.  2. Music—Analysis, appreciation.
I.  Title.
MT6.K877G7   Class suppl: MT6.K877G7Suppl.   781   75–40207
ISBN 0–393–09185–6 (Anthology I)

Book design by Hermann Strohbach

Printed in the United States of America

3 4 5 6 7 8 9

# CONTENTS

# GRADUS

## MUSIC ANTHOLOGY

## BOOK I

# 1

## Red River Valley

USA

From this val - ley they say you are go - ing,___ We will miss your bright eyes and sweet

smile, For they say you are tak - ing the sun - shine, That bright - ens our path - way a while.

# 2

## Spanish Is the Loving Tongue

USA

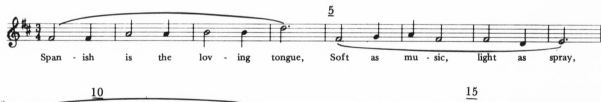

Span - ish is the lov - ing tongue, Soft as mu - sic, light as spray,

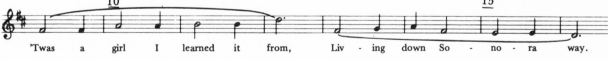

'Twas a girl I learned it from, Liv - ing down So - no - ra way.

I don't look much like a lov - er, Yet I say her loved words o - ver,

Of - ten when I'm all a - lone: "Mi a - mor, mi co - ra - zon."

1

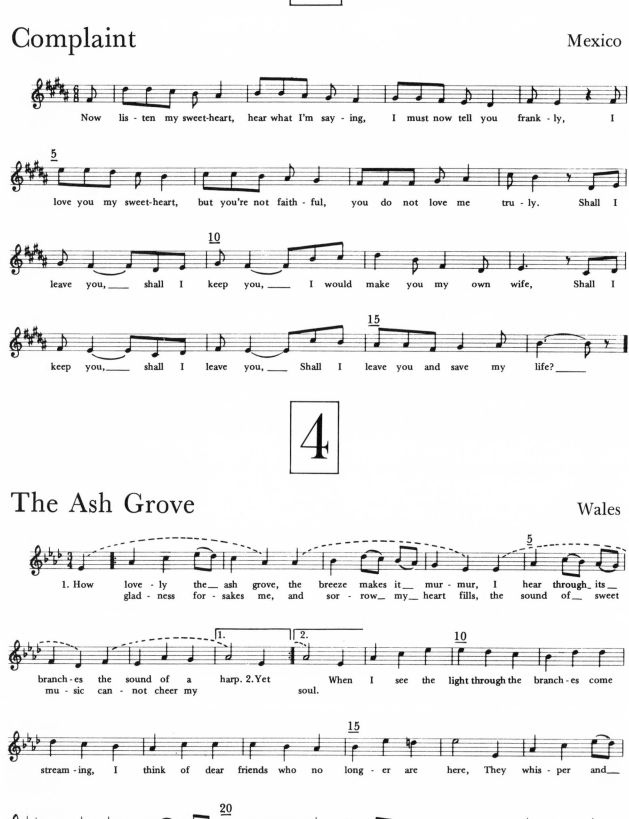

# 3

## Complaint

Mexico

Now lis - ten my sweet-heart, hear what I'm say - ing, I must now tell you frank - ly, I love you my sweet-heart, but you're not faith - ful, you do not love me tru - ly. Shall I leave you,___ shall I keep you,___ I would make you my own wife, Shall I keep you,___ shall I leave you,___ Shall I leave you and save my life?____

# 4

## The Ash Grove

Wales

1. How love - ly the__ ash grove, the breeze makes it__ mur - mur, I hear through__ its__
   glad - ness for - sakes me, and sor - row__ my__ heart fills, the sound of__ sweet

branch - es the sound of a harp. 2. Yet When I see the light through the branch - es come
mu - sic can - not cheer my soul.

stream - ing, I think of dear friends who no long - er are here, They whis - per and__

mur - mur, their mem - 'ry__ is __ mu - sic, The ash grove__ sings__ soft - ly of those who are gone.

# 5

## The Vicar of Bray

England

In good King Charles's gold-en days, When loy-al-ty no crime meant, A zeal-ous__ High Church-

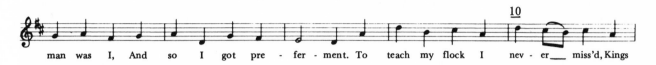

man was I, And so I got pre-fer-ment. To teach my flock I nev-er__ miss'd, Kings

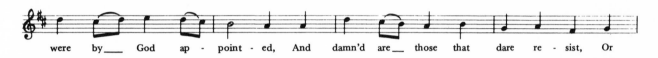

were by__ God ap-point-ed, And damn'd are__ those that dare re-sist, Or

touch the Lord's an-noint-ed, And this is__ law that I'll main-tain, Un-til my__ dy-ing__

day, sir, That what-so-ev-er king may reign, Still I'll be the Vi-car of Bray, sir.

# 6

## The Violet

Spain

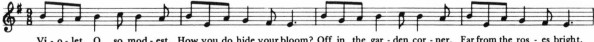

Vi-o-let, O, so mod-est, How you do hide your bloom? Off in the gar-den cor-ner, Far from the ros-es bright.

Try-ing to be un-no-ticed, try-ing to hide your face, Your love-ly scent re-veals you, Tells me your hid-ing place.

# 7

## Wedding Song

Greece

'Tis time__ to start__ the__ wed - ding, don't be re - luc - tant__ now. 'Tis__

time for you__ to__ mar - ry, So we can drink__ and__ dance. 'Tis__ dance.

I don't want__ to, I don't want to, Can't we all__ do__ some - thing else?

Drink with - out__ me, dance with - out me, I will nev - er__ wed.____

All your friends are__ here, __ And the bride is wait - ing for__ you, You must mar - ry__ now.__

# 8

## Love Song

Central America

I see your__ face in a flow - ing stream, the sun - shines high__ a - bove.____

Clouds come and cov - er the sun, the wind blows__ loud __ and shrill,

Dark - ness has come and where is my love.____ Come, sun and shine __ on me.

# 9

## Young Man's Song

Hungary

What a girl, is my girl, Pret - ti - er than an - y.. Hap - py me,
luck - y me, hap - pi - er than an - y. Ap - ples grow, peach - es grow,
ev - 'ry - where you look, But, no-where else is a girl, who's as sweet as my girl.

# 10

## Nobody Knows the Trouble I've Seen

USA

No - bod - y knows the trou - ble I've seen,__ No - bod - y knows my sor - row,

*Fine*

No - bod - y knows the trou - ble I've seen,__ Glo - ry, Hal - le - lu - jah! Some - times I'm up, some -

*D. C. al Fine*

times I'm down, Oh yes, Lord, Some - times I'm al - most to the ground, Oh, yes, Lord.

# 11

## Revival Song

USA

Sin - ner please don't let this har - vest pass,_____ Sin - ner

please don't let this har - vest pass, har - vest pass,\_\_\_ Sin - ner please don't\_

let this har - vest pass, And die and lose\_ your soul at last._____

# 12

## Song of the Sentry

Japan

**Voice**

**Koto**

Why can I not rest? Birds fly - ing past my\_ guard house

must dis - turb\_ my sleep.

(Suggestion of bird's flight)

No, it is not the\_ bird cries Sor - row dis - turbs my heart, my rest.

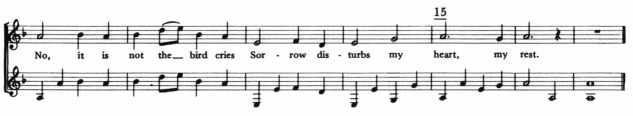

An example of heterophony. Two somewhat different versions of the same melody are heard simultaneously, without too much regard for the clashes that result.

# Countryland

Sweden

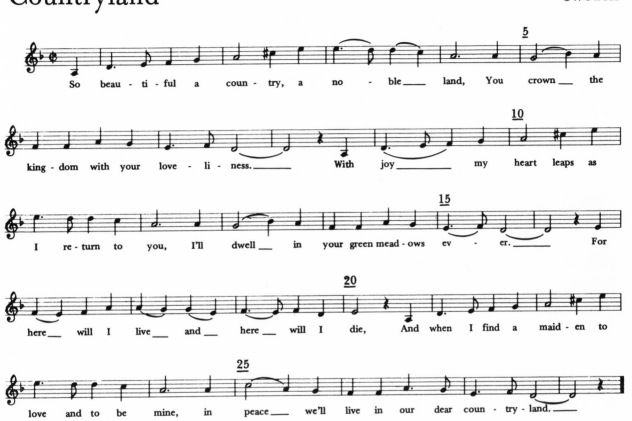

So beau - ti - ful a coun - try, a no - ble land, You crown the king - dom with your love - li - ness. With joy my heart leaps as I re - turn to you, I'll dwell in your green mead - ows ev - er. For here will I live and here will I die, And when I find a maid - en to love and to be mine, in peace we'll live in our dear coun - try - land.

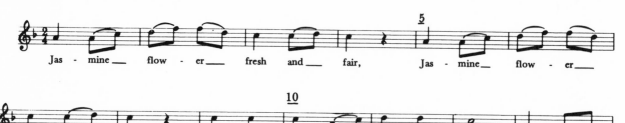

## Jasmine Flower

China

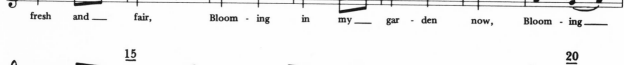

Jas - mine __ flow - er __ fresh and __ fair, Jas - mine __ flow - er __

fresh and __ fair, Bloom - ing in my __ gar - den now, Bloom - ing __

in my __ gar - den __ now. I __ would __ nev - er part from __ you,

Bring good __ luck __ to __ me, jas - mine, bring good luck __ to __ me.

## Soldier's Song

Hungary

I am call'd up to the col - ors, I'm to be a sol - dier, No use cry - ing,

no use weep - ing, I'm to be a sol - dier. Stop your sil - ly tears, now, noth - ing we can

do now, Love must soon come to an end for I must do my du - ty.

8

# 16

## Haul Away, Joe

USA

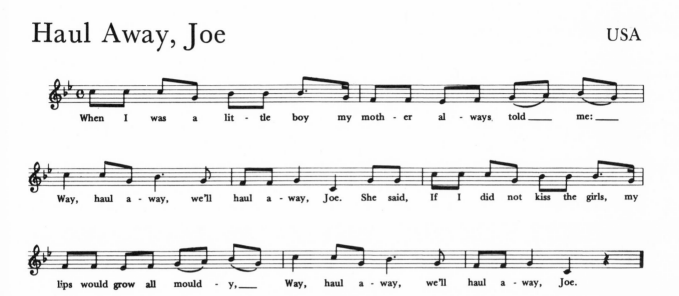

When I was a lit - tle boy my moth - er al - ways told \_\_\_ me: \_\_

Way, haul a - way, we'll haul a - way, Joe. She said, If I did not kiss the girls, my

lips would grow all mould - y, \_\_ Way, haul a - way, we'll haul a - way, Joe.

# 17

## Sabbath Hymn

Jewish

Peace, peace, grant\_ us\_ peace, grant\_ us\_ peace\_ and\_ bless - ing,\_ Peace, peace,

grant us\_ peace, on this Sab - bath day. And may it be your will, Lord to grant\_ us a bless - ing up-

on this Sab - bath day, For\_ in the light \_\_ of \_\_ Thy coun-te-nance, peace and bless - ing dwell.

*Fine*

*Da Capo al Fine*

# 18

## Go Away, John

My daugh-ter has been ab-sent, John, and has-n't been seen to-day, ____ And if she were here, John, she'd cast you far a-way. My daugh-ter's ver-y rich, John, and you are ver-y poor, You'd bet-ter seek your lodg-ing in some oth-er store.

# 19

## Tarantella

Italy

Ev-'ry eve-ning I go danc-ing, I go danc-ing by__ the sea, If by chance my sweet-heart joins me I'm as hap-py as can be. As__ we dance__ the tar-an-tel-la we__ all leap__ and kick__ and prance, All the vil-lag-ers will come and join__ the live-ly jump-ing dance, Ev-'ry-bod-y will be mer-ry as__ a-round the fire__ we dance.

# 20

## Merry Song

Romania

We go danc-ing, we go sing-ing, Vi-o-lin is mad-ly ring-ing, Ev-'ry-one is danc-ing,spring-ing,

glass-es full and friends are sing-ing, Hey!__ play the fid - dle, Dance,__ sing,__ play,__ jump,__

Hey!__ all the lads here laugh,__ dance,__ jump,__ strut,__ Hey!__ all the girls here,

Smile,__ dance,__ wink,__ nod,__ Hey!__ all the night we dance,__ sing,__ play,__ laugh.__

# 21

## The Pines

Czechoslovakia

Fra - grant pine trees ev - er green, tow - 'ring trees that I a - dore,

Here my lov - er__ came to join me, But he comes__ nev - er more.__

# Plainchant

Vic - ti - mae pas - cha - li lau - des im - mo - lent Chri - sti - a - ni Ag - nus re - de - mit o - ves

Chri - stus in - no - cens Pa - tri re - con - ci - li - a - vit pec - ca - to - res.

Va - do ad e - um qui mi - sit___ me e - ne - mo ex vo - bis in - ter -

ro - gat me Quo___ va - dis? Al - le - lu - ia,___ Al - le - lu - ia.

Ky - ri - e e - le - i - son Ky - ri - e e___ e - le - i - son

Ky - ri - e e - le - i - son.

Ky - ri - e___ e - - - - le - i - son Chri - ste e - -

- - - le - i - son Ky - ri - e___ e - - - - le - i - son

An organ setting of this chant may be found in 26 .

Di - es i - rae, di - es il - la, Sol - vet___ sae - clum___ in fa - vi - la:

Tes - te___ Da - vid___ cum Sy - byl - la.

This melody appears in the last movement of the *Fantastic Symphony* by Hector Berlioz, and in the *Variations on a Theme of Paganini* by Sergei Rachmaninov.

Glo - ri - a___ in ex - cel - sis De - o et in ter - ra pax ho - mi - ni - bus bo - nae vo - lun - ta - tae.

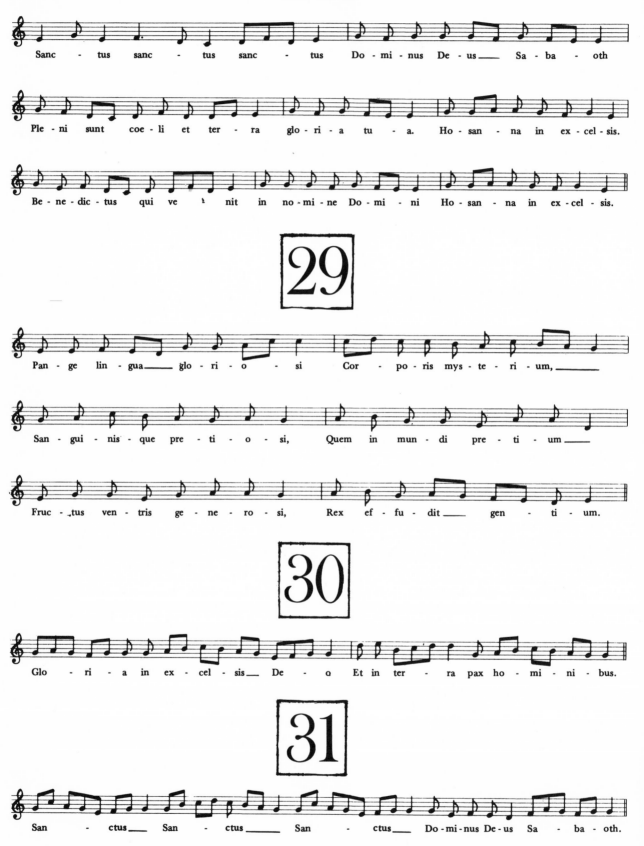

**28**

Sanc - tus sanc - tus sanc - tus Do - mi - nus De - us___ Sa - ba - oth

Ple - ni sunt coe - li et ter - ra glo - ri - a tu - a. Ho - san - na in ex - cel - sis.

Be - ne - dic - tus qui ve - nit in no - mi - ne Do - mi - ni Ho - san - na in ex - cel - sis.

**29**

Pan - ge lin - gua___ glo - ri - o - si Cor - po - ris mys - te - ri - um, ___

San - gui - nis - que pre - ti - o - si, Quem in mun - di pre - ti - um ___

Fruc - tus ven - tris ge - ne - ro - si, Rex ef - fu - dit ___ gen - ti - um.

**30**

Glo - ri - a in ex - cel - sis___ De - o Et in ter - ra pax ho - mi - ni - bus.

**31**

San - ctus___ San - ctus___ San - ctus___ Do - mi - nus De - us Sa - ba - oth.

**32**

Cre - do in u - num De - o  Pa - trem om - ni - po - ten - tem  Fac - to - rem coe - li et ter - rae

vi - si - bi - li - um om - ni - um _____ et in - vi - si - bi - li - um.

**33**

Ve - ni  Cre - a - tor ____ Spi - ri - tus,  Men - tes tu - o - rum ____ vi - si - ta;

Im - ple - su - per - na ___ gra - ti - a.  Quae tu cre - as - ti _____ pec - to - ra.

**34**

Ag - nus  De - i ____ qui ____ tol - lis pec - ca - ta mun - di

mi - se - re - re ____ no - bis.

**35**

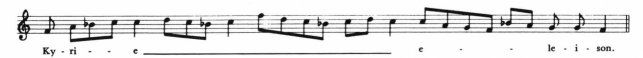

Ky - ri - e _____ e - - le - i - son.

# 36

## Hebrew Cantillation

And the earth _____ was un-form'd and void,_ and dark - ness was up - on the face _ of the deep; and the spir - it of God_ hov - er'd o - ver the face of the wa - ters.

# 37

## Armenian Chant

The _ ce - les - tial choirs _____ sing _____ with _ us this _____ day,

For _ this _ day _ we re - mem - ber ho - ly Saint Ste - phen,

Glo - ri - fy - ing, Thee, _____ O _____

Lord, _____ God _____ of our _____ fa - thers, our God.

# Bicinium

Kaspar Othmayr 1547

A might-y for-tress is ___ our ___ God, A good-ly ___

1    3      5   6   6    3   ②   6   ⑦   6    8

A might-y for-tress is ___ our God, A good-ly

shield ___ and wea - - pon. The old and e - - vil foe,

shield and wea - - pon. The old ___ and e - - vil foe,

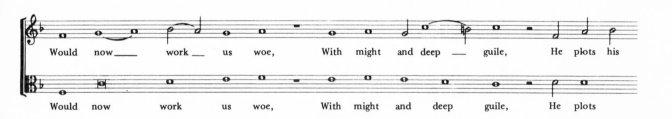

Would now ___ work ___ us woe, With might and deep ___ guile, He plots his

Would now work us woe, With might and deep guile, He plots

wick - - ed way, There's none on earth so e - - - - vil.

his wick - - ed way, There's none on earth so e - - vil.

# 39

**Duo** from *Springtime*                                      Claude Le Jeune   1603

How the wa-ter in the stream flows, ___ Seek-ing Sum-mer's riv - er to join,

How the wa-ter in ___ the_ stream _ flows, Seek-ing Sum-mer's riv - er to ___ join,

And the calm sur - face of ___ its waves, Bright-ens ev - 'ry shad - y cor - ner.

And the calm sur - face of its waves, ___ Bright-ens ev - 'ry shad - y cor - ner.

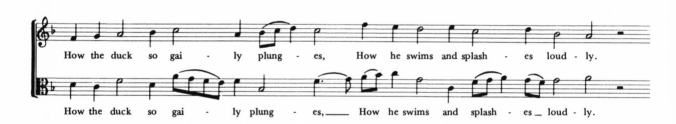

How the duck so gai - ly plung - es, How he swims and splash - es loud - ly.

How the duck so gai - ly plung - es, ___ How he swims and splash - es _ loud - ly.

And the crane ___ takes wing and flies off, Flies a - way in - to ___ the Spring - time.

And the crane ___ takes wing ___ and flies off, Flies a - way in - to the Spring - time.

# Chanson

Jacques Arcadelt    1554

Men all are such great lov-ers, Or so they do pro-claim, And wom-en are so fool-ish To put on Love the blame. But what seems right for men-folk For wom-en leads to shame, And mis-er-y soon fol-lows If we leave the path of Hon-or's path.

# 41

# Et incarnatus est

from the Mass *Pange Lingua*

Josquin des Pres   c. 1500

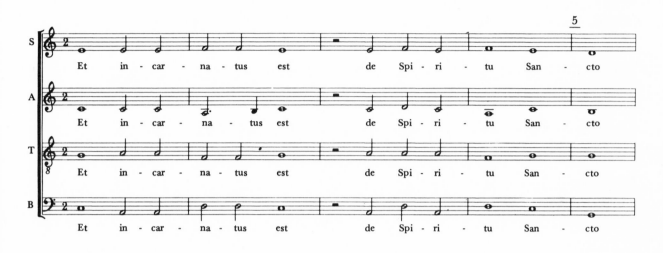

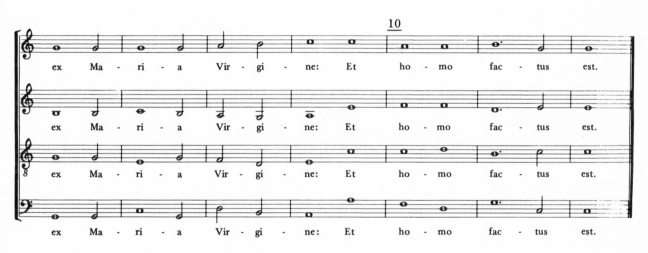

# 42

# In Maytime

Ludwig Senfl   1544

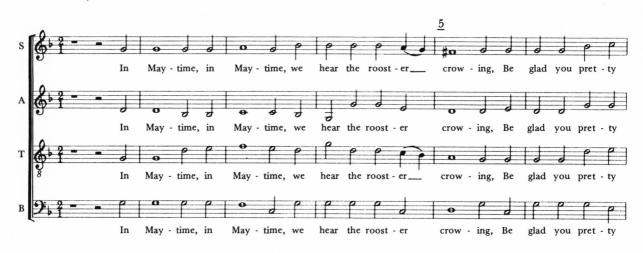

# Psalm 61

Melody by Louis Bourgeois
Setting by Claude Goudimel   1565

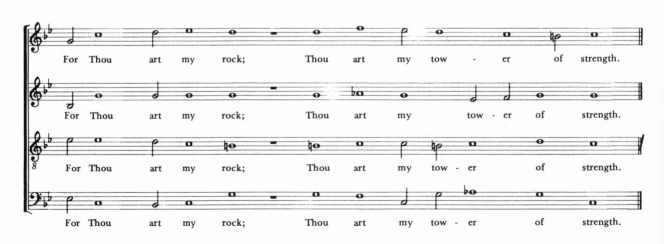

# Psalm 78

Heinrich Schütz  1628

People, give ear un-to my law, Heark-en to all I say to you,

People, give ear un-to my law, Heark-en to all I say to you,

People, give ear un-to my law, Heark-en to all I say to you,

People, give ear un-to my law, Heark-en to all I say to you,

For I will tell you strange things, I will now lift my voice in song,

For I will tell you strange things, I will now lift my voice in song,

For I will tell you strange things, I will now lift my voice in song,

For I will tell you strange things, I will now lift my voice in song,

I tell what we have heard and known, Tale that our fa-thers told _____ us.

I tell what we have heard and known, Tale that our fa-thers told _____ us.

I tell what we have heard and known, Tale that our fa-thers told _____ us.

I tell what we have heard and known, Tale that our fa-thers told us.

# 45

## Innsbruck,
## I Now Must Leave Thee

Heinrich Isaac   c. 1500

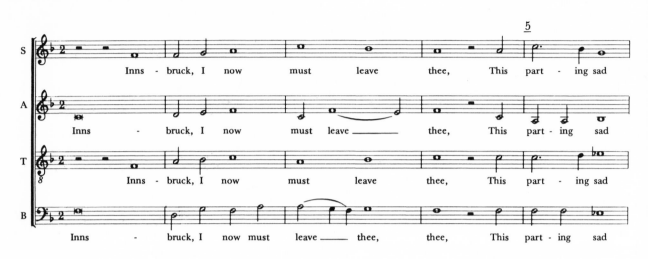

Inns - bruck, I now must leave thee, This part - ing sad

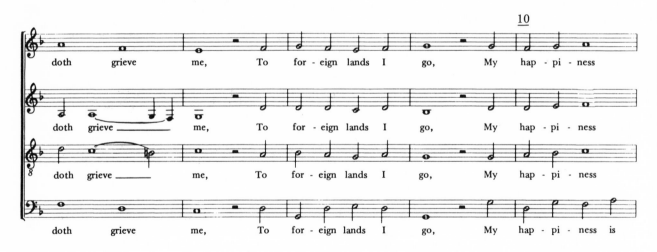

doth grieve me, To for - eign lands I go, My hap - pi - ness

is end - ed, I nev - er will re - gain it, I

# Festive Song

Baldassare Donati    1551

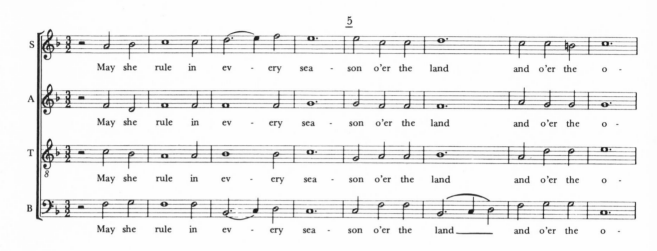

May she rule in ev - ery sea - son o'er the land and o'er the o -

ceans, And may great Lib - er - ty flour - ish, O great Queen of all the na -

tions. In all times and in all plac - es, May her pow - er grow for - ev -

er, So that all____ men may cry out: Long life to Ve - nice, Long life to Ve - nice,

er, So that all____ men may cry out: Long life to Ve - nice, Long life to Ve - nice,

er, So that all____ men may cry out: Long life to Ve - nice, Long life to Ve - nice,

er, So that all men may cry out: Long life to Ve - nice, Long life to Ve - nice,

Queen of all. Long life to Ve - nice, Long life to Ve - nice, Queen of all.

Queen of all. Long life to Ve - nice, Long life to Ve - nice, Queen of all.

Queen_ of all. Long life to Ve - nice, Long life to Ve - nice, Queen_ of all.

Queen_ of all. Long life to Ve - nice, Long life to Ve - nice, Queen_ of all.

# Good Day, My Heart

Orlando di Lasso   c. 1575

Good day my heart, Good day my dar - ling, my _____ sweet life!
Good day my eye, Good day my ver - y dear - est love!

Good day my heart, Good day my dar - ling sweet life!
Good day my eye, Good day my ver - y dear love!

Good day my heart, Good day dar - ling, my sweet life!
Good day my eye, Good day my ver - y dear love!

Good day my heart, Good day my dar - ling, my sweet life!
Good day my eye, Good day my ver - y dear love!

Ah! Good day my lit - tle pret - ty, My charm-ing sweet one, Good __ day you who

Ah! Good day my lit - tle pret - ty, My charm-ing sweet one, Good __ day you who

Ah! Good day my lit - tle pret - ty, My charm-ing sweet one, Good __ day you who

Ah! Good day my lit - tle pret - ty, My charm-ing sweet one, Good __ day you who

bring de - light and love, My gen - tle Spring, my love - ly flow - er in bloom, My

bring de - light and love, My gen - tle Spring, my love - ly flow - er in bloom, My

bring de - light and love, My gen - tle Spring, my love - ly flow - er in bloom, My

bring de - light and love, My gen - tle Spring, my love - ly flow - er in bloom, My

pleas-ure sweet,my gen-tle lit-tle soft dove, My lit-tle bird, My lit-tle tur-tle dove, dear, Good

pleas-ure sweet,my gen-tle lit-tle soft dove, My lit-tle bird, My lit-tle tur-tle dove, dear, Good

pleas-ure sweet,my gen-tle lit-tle soft dove, My lit-tle bird, My lit-tle tur-tle dove, my dear, Good

pleas-ure sweet,my gen-tle lit-tle soft dove, My lit-tle dove, My lit-tle tur-tle dove, dear, Good

_ day my sweet lit-tle re-bel, Good day my sweet lit-tle re-bel.

_ day my sweet lit-tle re-bel, Good_ day_ my_ sweet_ lit-tle re-bel.

_ day my sweet lit-tle re-bel, Good_ day my_ sweet lit-tle re-bel.

_ day my sweet lit-tle re-bel, Good day my_ sweet lit-tle re-bel.

A facsimile of the canto part of *Love's Pursuit* by Giovanni Gastoldi from the late 16th century edition.

# Love's Pursuit

Ballata "To be sung, played, and danced"                    Giovanni Gastoldi    1591

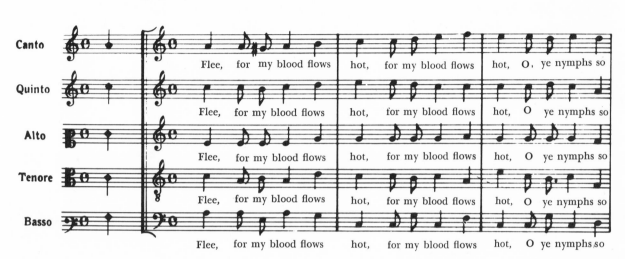

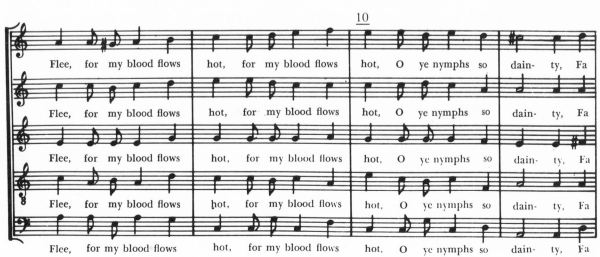

In this and all other examples where the text has been translated for this volume, the original flags and beams have been retained.

# Allemande

Claude Gervaise  1550

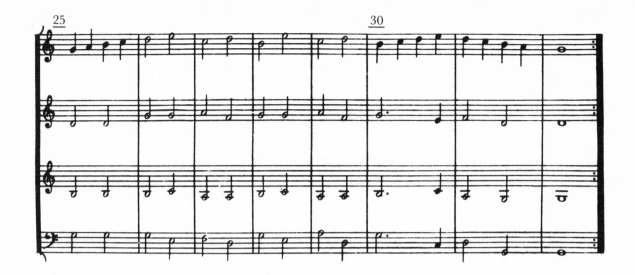

# 49B

## Bransle de Poictou

Claude Gervaise    1550

# 50A

## Gaillarde

Michael Praetorius   1620

# 50B

## Courante

Michael Praetorius   1620

## Two Sarabandes

Michael Praetorius    1620

# 51A

## No. 32: In Dorian Mode

from *Mikrokosmos*

Béla Bartók   1936

# 51B

## No. 34: In Phrygian Mode
from *Mikrokosmos*

Béla Bartók  1936

# No. 51: Waves from *Mikrokosmos*

Béla Bartók 1936

# 51D

## No. 58: In Oriental Style

from *Mikrokosmos*

Béla Bartók    1936

# No. 59: Major and Minor

from *Mikrokosmos*

Béla Bartók   1936

# Between the Earth and Sky

from *Quatrains Valaisans* by Rainer Maria Rilke          Darius Milhaud    1940

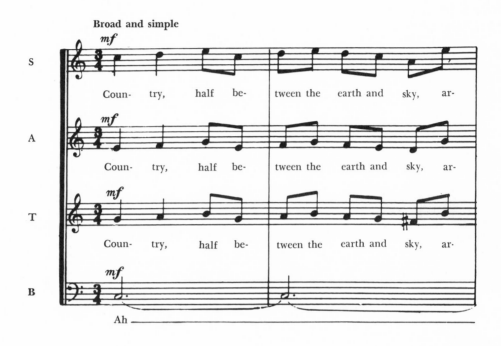

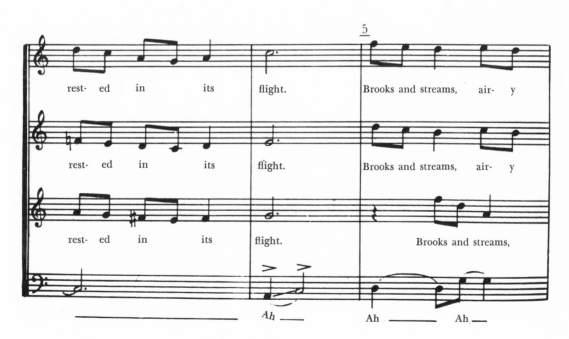

46

# Symphony for Strings

second movement, mm. 1–19

William Schuman    1943

# 54

## Story of Our Town

from *Our Town Suite*

Aaron Copland    1940

# A Swan

from the French of Rainer Maria Rilke

Paul Hindemith   1943

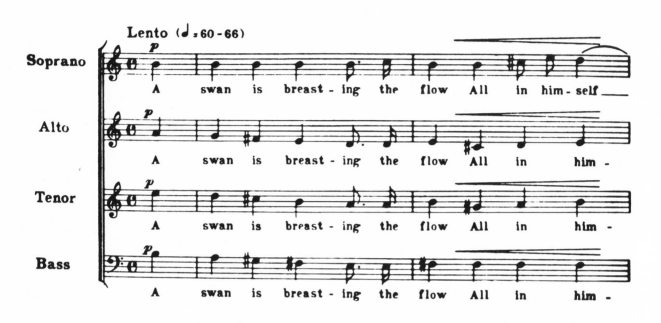

51

# 56

# March from *Renard**

Igor Stravinsky    1918

\* Reduced score by Leo Kraft.

By Permission of J. & W. Chester. Edition Wilhelm Hansen London, Ltd.

53

# Chaconne (excerpt)

Johann Pachelbel    1700

# 58

**Duet** from *Come, Ye Sons of Art*    Henry Purcell  1694

# Passacaglia  from Suite No. 7

George Frideric Handel  1720

# 60

## Gavotte and Variations

Jean-Philippe Rameau    1736

**1.ᵉʳ Double**

2.<sup>me</sup> Double

3.<sup>me</sup> Double

4me Double

5<sup>me</sup> Double

6<sup>me</sup> Double

## Pavana

William Byrd    late 16th century

# Recitative from Cantata No. 60

Johann Sebastian Bach    1723

**RECITATIVE**

will all my sins and my great guilt be reck-oned up a-gainst me

And for that rea-son God will not pro- death's Here is an
nounce judg-ment!

6
4
2

7
#

6

7♭

20 (Arioso.)

end to all temp-ta-tion's tor-ment That we may gain sal- va-

25

- - - - - - - tion.

70

# Organ Toccata in E Minor

Johann Pachelbel    1700

# 64

## Toccata from *Fiori Musicali*

Girolamo Frescobaldi 1635

# 65

**Plein Jeu**

Nicholas de Grigny    1700

# 66

Mein junges Leben hat ein End'          J. P. Sweelinck   c. 1625

# Kyrie  from *Fiori Musicali*

Girolamo Frescobaldi    1635

# 68

## Charlie Is My Darling

Scottish Folk Song
Arranged by Ludwig van Beethoven    1815

# 69A

## In Quiet Night

German Folk Song
Arranged by Johannes Brahms

**Fairly slow**

SOPRANO: In qui-et night, when all is still, I hear a sad voice sing-ing, The wind of night brings

ALTO: In qui-et night, when all is still, I hear a sad voice sing-ing, The wind of night brings

TENOR: In qui-et night, when all is still, I hear a sad voice sing-ing, The wind of night brings

BASS: In qui-et night, when all is still, voice sing-ing, The wind of night brings

soft to me its mel-an-chol-y ring-ing; And when I hear that voice a- rise, my

soft to me its mel-an-chol y ring-ing; And when I hear that voice a- rise, my

soft to me its mel-an-chol-y ring-ing; And when I hear that voice a- rise, my

soft to me its mel-an-chol-y ring-ing; And when I hear that voice a- rise, my

heart is fill'd with sad-ness, The lit- tle flow'rs, the fair-est blooms, are cov-er'd with my tear drops.

heart is fill'd with sad-ness, The lit- tle flow'rs, the fair-est blooms, are cov-er'd with my tear drops.

heart is fill'd with sad-ness, The lit- tle flow'rs, the fair- est blooms, are cov-er'd with my tear drops.

heart is\fill'd with sad-ness, The lit- tle flow'rs, the fair- est blooms, are cov-er'd with my tear drops.

# How Darkly the Water Flows

German Folk Song
Arranged by Johannes Brahms    1864

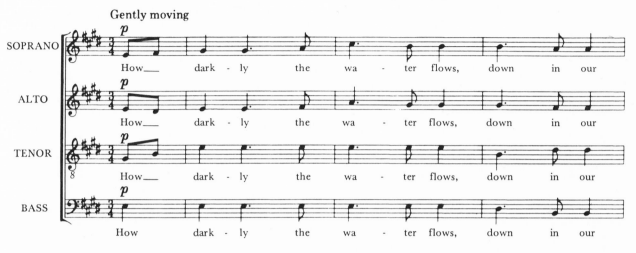

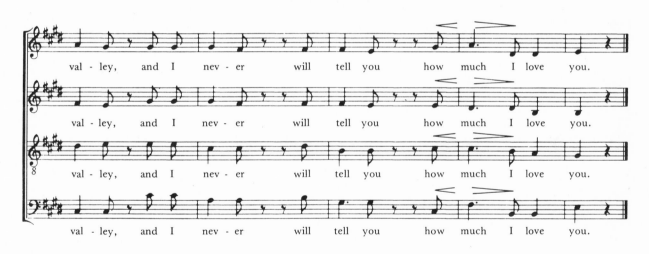

# Love Song

German Folk Song
Arranged by Johannes Brahms    1864

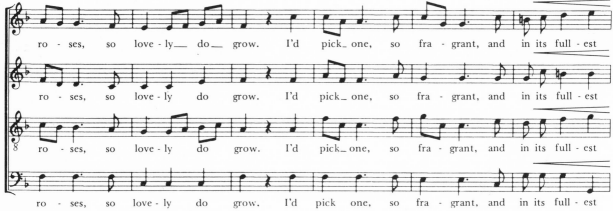

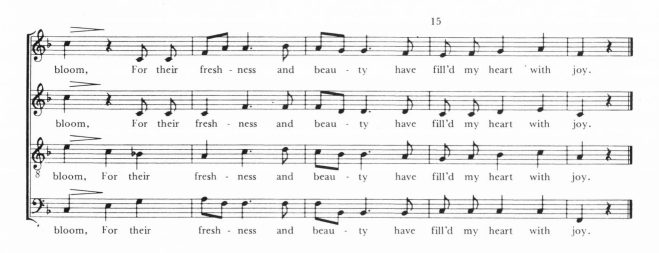

# 70A

## How Darkly the Water Flows

German Folk Song
Arranged by Johannes Brahms

# I Love a Charming Brunette

German Folk Song
Arranged by Johannes Brahms

**With movement and expression**

1. I love a charm-ing sweet bru-nette, if on-ly she lov'd
2. I'd serve that love-ly maid-en well, I'd serve her all my

me. Would God I could be with her now, and she would be with
life. If on-ly she would love me too, and be my lit- tle

me. I have no peace by day or night when
wife. On earth there's noth- ing I de- sire, but

# 70C

## Love Song

German Folk Song
Arranged by Johannes Brahms

O maid - en, O maid - en, in your gar - den_ I'd_ go, To see_ how the ros - es so love - ly_ do_ grow. I'd pick_ one, so fra - grant, and in its full - est bloom, For their fresh - ness and beau - ty have fill'd my heart with joy.

# Russian Folk Song

Arranged by N. Rimsky-Korsakov 1877

Peter Tchaikovsky used this melody in the Finale of his *Fourth Symphony*.

# Secondo

## Five Russian Folk Songs

Arranged by P. I. Tchaikovsky

This is the melody of the Finale to *The Firebird,* by Igor Stravinsky.

# Five Russian Folk Songs

Arranged by P. I. Tchaikovsky

This tune figures prominently in the Third Tableau of *Petrushka,* by Igor Stravinsky.

This is the melody of the Finale to *The Firebird,* by Igor Stravinsky.

# Secondo

## 72C

## 72D

## 72E

## 72C

Tchaikovsky used this tune again in the last movement of his *Serenade for Strings.*

## 72D

This is the melody of the second movement of Tchaikovsky's *String Quartet No. 1.*

## 72E

# Hungarian Folk Song

Arranged by Béla Bartók    1908

# Snow Flakes

Arranged by Sergei Prokofiev    1962

slow-ly I ____ shed tears ____ a- lone, Tears will

dry up, snow will melt, ____ Grass ____ will

grow ____ up- on the plain.

# Piano Sonata No. 3, page 1       Norman Dello Joio    1947

# Fortress, Rock of Our Salvation

Hebrew Folk Song
Arranged by Hugo Weisgall   1957

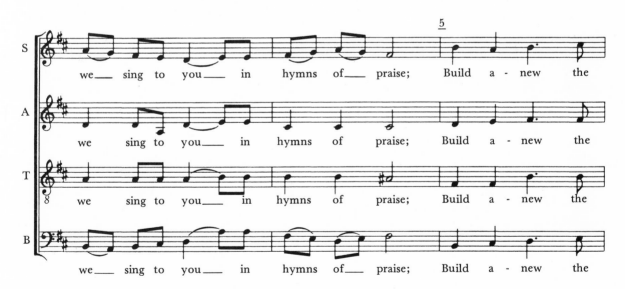

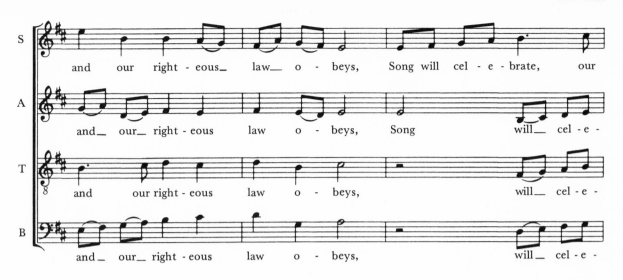

# 77

# Simple Gifts

Arranged by Aaron Copland  1950

Copland's variations on this melody form the latter part of the ballet score *Appalachian Spring*.

# 78

## Bon Jour Mõ Cueur Di Orlando

from the *Fitzwilliam Virginal Book*                    Peter Philips    1602

# To Doris, Ode for Voice and Continuo

G. M. Telemann 1741

Now first I learn to know your soul, Which I so long have lov'd and still love

Now can I say to all temp-ta- tions, That they mean noth-ing to my glad heart;

Now can no need op- press my sens- es, En- vy and long -ing are now dead

I need but think of my good for- tune, That you are mine is my life's joy.

# 79B

## To Sleep, Ode for Voice and Continuo

G. M. Telemann    1741

God of dream-ing, friend of Night! Cause of sweet- est pleas- ure! No- ble

You who bring the hum-ble rest, when the Lord op-pres- ses.

Mor-pheus tar- ries not, When he bears all-heal- ing peace, Eye and heart, to com- fort. fort.

# 79C

# Plain Cooking,
## Ode for Voice and Continuo

G. M. Telemann   1741

# Bourée from *Dance Pieces*

J. P. Kirnberger   c. 1760

PIECES DE CLAVECIN

en Deux Volumes

Consistant des

Ouvertures, Preludes, Fugues, Allemandes,
Courentes, Sarabandes, Giques, et Aires.

Composées

par

J. Mattheson.

Secr.

17  14.

The title page of the original edition in which the Mattheson *Sarabandes* appeared, London, 1714.

# Sarabande and Double

Johann Mattheson    1714

Reprint of the edition of 1713.

# 81B

## Sarabande

Johann Mattheson 1714

# 82

## La Lugubre

from *The First Order of Harpsichord Pieces*

François Couperin    1713

# 83

## Allemande  from French Suite No. 1    Johann Sebastian Bach   c. 1720

# 84

## Violin Sonata in A Minor,
**fourth movement**

Johann Sebastian Bach   c. 1720

# 85

**Minuet** from French Suite No. 6             Johann Sebastian Bach    c. 1720

# 86

Air  from Suite No. 3 for Orchestra                Johann Sebastian Bach   c. 1720

# 87

## Sonata in D

Domenico Scarlatti   1739

From an edition printed in London in or around 1739. D means right hand, M means left hand. The flat sign means natural (flatten) when applied to the sharped notes in the key signature. The natural sign is used to cancel other sharps.

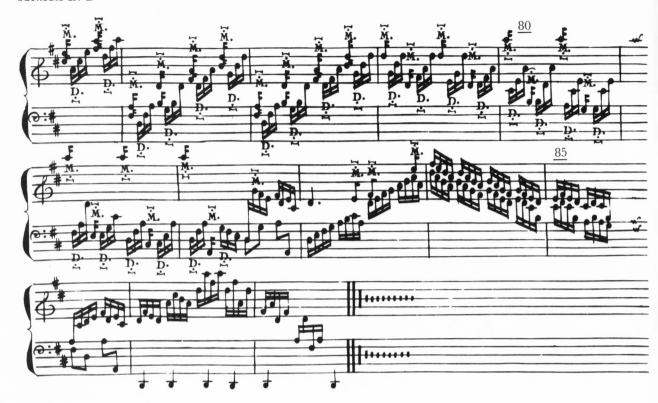

# 88

# Sonata for Violin and Continuo,
Op. 5 No. 5, Adagio

Arcangelo Corelli   c. 1700

# 89

**Trio Sonata** Op. 4 No. 2, Preludio                    Arcangelo Corelli    1700

## Cantabile from the *Table Music*

G. M. Telemann 1733

# 90B

## Andante from the *Table Music*

G. M. Telemann 1733

# 90C

## Largo from the *Table Music*

G. M. Telemann 1733

# Concerto Op. 6 No. 4, first movement George Frideric Handel 1739

# 92

## Concerto grosso
Op. 3 No. 8, first movement

Antonio Vivaldi    1715

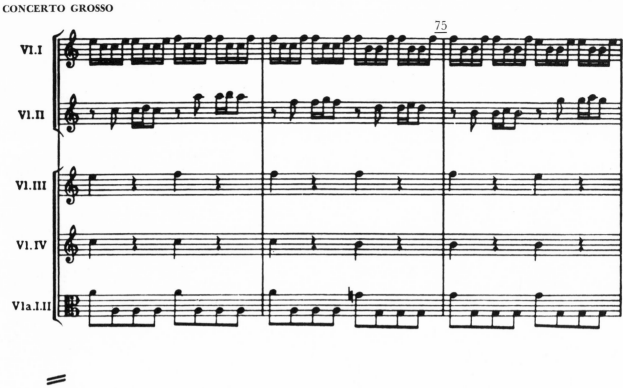

# Recitative and Aria

from *Flavio*

George Frideric Handel    1723

# Aria

*(Fine)*

*Da Capo.*

# Two-Part Organum  (excerpt)

Leonin   12th century

# 95

## Conductus

Notre Dame school   c. 1200

De _____

ca - sti - ta - tis tha - la - mo

Ven - trem vir - gi - na - lem   Pa - ter de - dit Fi - li - o   Val - lem spe - ci -

a - lem.   In - ve - ni - re po - te - rat   Quis in mun - do ta - lem

Ut por - ta - ret Fi - li - um   Pa - tri co - e - qua - - - - - - -

- - - - - - - - - - - - - - - - - lem.

**96**

# Conductus (opening section)

Perotin c. 1225

T: Sal - va - to - ris ho - di - e _____

B: Sal - va - to - ris ho - di - e _____

B: Sal - va - to - ris ho - di - e _____

_____ San - guis pre - gu -

_____ San - guis pre - gu -

_____ San - guis pre - gu -

sta - - - - - - - - -

sta - - - - - - - - -

sta - - - - - - - - -

- - - tur, In quo ___ Sy - on ___ Fi - li -

- - - tur, In quo Sy - on ___ Fi - li -

- - - tur, In quo ___ Sy - on Fi - li -

# 97

## Motet

Guillaume de Machaut    14th century

S: Heart de-nies it, my judg-ment too de-nies it, but they say___ that I en-joy___ the pleas - ures of sweet_ Love.

A: Sad - ness and un-hap-pi-ness so great! Would that I had some com - fort.

Inst.

S: They say that I do not tell the truth at all _____ When I _____ sing of my _____ pain, and that I real-ly

A: Would _ I had _____ some sol - ace now. Sad - - ness in the midst

S: do re-joice_ in _ the de-lights_ of gen - tle_ Love. A - las! for not a

A: of hap - - - i - ness, Mel - an - chol - - - -

S: day goes by which does not end in grief _____ For the La - dy whom I love in faith

A: - - y, I _ pass _ ev - 'ry day _____ and _ night,

She — to whom I be-long with all my soul. Her cold heart — is such an en-e-my

love and hon - or, I am — be-reft may Love help me!

That tru - ly it de-lights in the e-vil which it does to me. — I can see in-deed that I have failed.

But — up - on my soul, I lie in my teeth.

# 98

# Ballata

Francesco Landini   c. 1375

find peace on - ly when I think of you.

find peace on - ly when I think of you.

---

# 99

## Magnificat (excerpt)

Guillaume Dufay    c. 1450

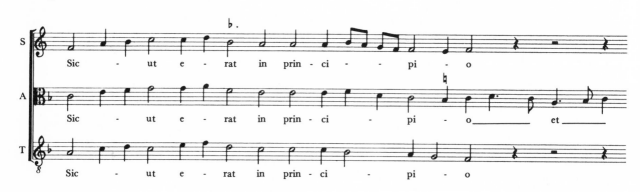

S: Sic - ut e - rat in prin - ci - pi - o

A: Sic - ut e - rat in prin - ci - pi - o___ et___

T: Sic - ut e - rat in prin - ci - pi - o

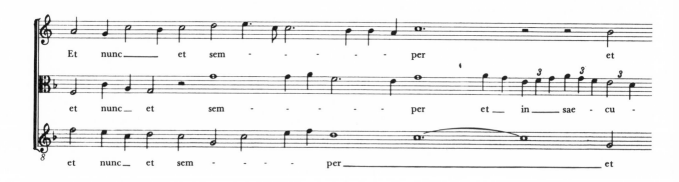

Et nunc___ et sem - per et

et nunc__ et sem - per et__ in___ sae - cu -

et nunc__ et sem - per___ et

in sae - cu - la sae - cu - lo - rum. A - men.

la sae - cu - lo - rum. A - men.

in___ sae - cu - la sae - cu - lo - rum. A - men.

# INDEX